CAPTIVATING E

MW00442972

HOW TO WRITE CAPTIVATING BLOG POSTS THAT KEEP READERS COMING BACK FOR MORE

By

SCOTT PILES

Copyright © 2016

TABLE OF CONTENTS

LEGAL NOTES

result of both personal experience, as well as the experiences of others.

INTRODUCTION

The secret to blogging success is in the content. You want profit? Produce value for your readers. It's as simple as that. I'm always being bombarded with questions on how you can write content that keeps readers coming back for more. Remember, great content almost always generates more organic traffic to your blog/site.

You will see as you read on how exactly you can keep your readers engaged and I will share with you some great tips and tricks on how I myself have gained readers trust and generated more organic traffic. This is coming from someone who has years of experience in content marketing and blogging.

I have seen some amazing real results implementing most of these strategies and I know you will too. So what are you waiting for, start reading!

CHAPTER 1.

PICKING THE RIGHT TOPIC

Starting a blog today is much easier than it was in the years past. There has been high level of advancement in technology that can easily help you out these days. However, one of the challenges confronting some bloggers is how to get the right topic for their blog post.

For you to write a captivating blog posts, you need a topic. The right topic helps you to be focused. Your main goal of writing is to reach the point where your audience will seek you out in the multitude. So to make your blog a huge success, you need to come up with great content idea or topic that will attract your audience and turn them into loyal readers.

Picking that right topic can be very tough and challenging indeed. Blogging is the best form for writing your idea or about your thought on issues you know very well. A great post will not only gains respect and favor of the readers but it also makes it the blog SEO-friendly as well and make your reader to always come back to you.

TIPS TO CHOOSING THE RIGHT TOPIC:

Write about something that excites you, period!

Write about something you truly know.

If you're an Internet marketer and truly care and passionate about the profession, while don't you create your blog in that area and just write about it.

Don't select a topic simply because you think that a lot of people search for it. But select your topic because you know you have much more knowledge about it. I wish you all the best in choosing your blog topic.

Here are just a few ways to get you started and hopefully make things easier for you to come up with some quality topics to write about:

SOURCES TO GET IDEAS FOR YOUR TOPIC

FROM THE NEWS:

Depending on what your niche or interest is, you may be surprised by how many ideas you could come up with by keeping up with the news. Of course, getting ideas or topic from news will keep you updated in your niche. There are many news publications available, but here are a few to keep in mind:

CNN: You will get many topic ideas on a regular basis

Huffington Post: This is another great online news portal where you can get thousands of blog post ideas and build on them.

The Washington Post: Another reliable source of getting blog post topics or ideas for your blog.

etc

Social Media

Another area to get idea or topic is the social media; social media networks can be a powerful way to find fresh ideas on your niche that you could write about each week. By following the buzz in social media networks, you can find topics on what is hot, which can give you trending topics to think about. Here are some suggestions on who to keep an eye on in your social media networks:

- **Follow others that have a similar business to yours**
- **Follow those that you have determined to be your ideal clients/customers**
- **Follow others that are in a different niche than yours, but may have clients/customers that could be interested in your topics.**

GOOGLE ALERTS

Using Google Alerts is a very powerful resource in finding what topics are trending (this is surely the favorite option). The tool is especially useful because you can go in and sign up to receive daily or weekly emails showing what is being searched for and talked about online. Don't know about how to use Google alerts? Here is how you can get started with Google alerts:

- **Go to http://www.google.com/alerts**
- **Type in your search query (keywords related to your niche)**
- **Pick, if you want the alerts from Everything, News, Blogs, Video, Discussions and Books,**
- **Choose language and region**
- **Pick how often you want to receive the alerts**
- **Choose "Only the best results" or "All results"**
- **Input the email address you want the results sent to and you will be getting alerts from google on any trending area of your interest.**

Etc

Getting right topic for your blog post can be frustrating, but if you familiar yourself with some points mentioned above I can tell you your blogging experience will be engaging and rewarding one. And you will get tons of blog topics on a regular basis.

By using the strategies and resources above, I hope that you will find it easier to come up with the blog post topics you are looking for each time you are in need of fresh content. You can also get blog post topics from web 2.0, micro blogging sites, article directories and many more.

Now let us see how you will make your blog post friendly to search engine. Read more in the next chapter.

CHAPTER 2.

MAKING YOUR BLOG POST SEARCH ENGINE OPTIMIZED

You have a blog that filled with useful contents and you are updating it regularly and yet you are not getting traffic. But you are wondering why it's not attracting more visitors as it opt to be. This is a common problem with most new and even old bloggers and website owners. The solution is simple - you need to spend quality time optimizing it for search engine to gain organic traffic.

Thank God you are reading this section or chapter. Let me ask you this question: When you search for information on the search engines for either research work or trying to buy something, you search with keywords related to what you need. If your blog is about 'Make Money Online', you will need to find keyword phrases that searchers would be searching for that relates to make money online.

You will have to include in your content some keywords phrases that will make searchers locate you on the net. You will need to get relevant keywords phrase which can be done through Google keyword

Planner or you consult somebody to get relevant keywords for you at small bucks.

Once you have compiled a list of these keywords, you want to write the blog post topics based on them. Have the keywords appear in the post title at least once. The titles you write for the blog posts are very important, because the search engines put a lot of "weights" in this area. You need to think about the search engines as well as humans when writing blog post titles. Please let me advise you not to over use those keyword phrases in the content because Google will see it as keyword stuffing and you will be penalized.

If you are using Wordpress for your blog, you can use a SEO plugin like "Wordpress SEO by Yoast" or "All in SEO" to make the page title same as the post title automatically. This will greatly improve the ranking of the sub pages (blog posts).

As I said above, use the keywords you have gathered naturally within the content. Always learn to use related keywords as much as possible to support the main ones in the content. You must also put some of these keywords in the description.

The spiders and bots love these contents and now index them faster than normal websites. The short, regular posts contain lots of tasty keywords and easy-to-digest content.

RULES TO SEO (ON-PAGE SEO)

1. Use keywords in the Title,
2. Make sure your post contains relevant content with relevant keywords,
3. You description must contain some of those keywords
4. Keep it short - 350 - 500 words or less, but sometimes you can make it long especially if static page or unable to write often,
5. Blog post regularly because Google bots like fresh or new contents,
6. Use your brand name in every blog so that you will be known online
7. Optimize your use of keywords and long-tail keywords to avoid keyword stuffing
8. Choose a specific niche and stick to it.
9. Make sure the colors and logo you using are part of your brand family, so your blogs are easily recognizable.
10. Avoid Keywords stuffing as much as you can in your content.
11. Follow keyword density of 2-3% in your content.

Linking pages of your website to home page or to one another is an important part of search engine optimization and blogs are easy to link to each other.

The more relevant links you have, the higher you will be ranked. It will take time and a lot of effort to get to the top of the rankings, and there are other tricks you might find along the way.

CHAPTER 3.

PEOPLE LOVE FREE OFFERS

With so much business on the web, it is hard to obtain customers especially when you are selling items and even more difficult to have them return. But one proven and easy way of getting them to your web site is to offer a free gift for them.

When selling products or rendering services to people online, you have to do everything to attract new customers and also retain the existing/old customers.

All over the internet you will see different ads asking people for action for free gift. e.g. just for viewing receive your free gift, no strings attached, no obligation, etc. All these slogans are meant to catch people's attention.

You must offer a free gift up front to grab them. Everyone loves the word free and gift, adding those to words together is like magic. It draws people, it catches their curiosity, and it absorbs them. They can't help themselves.

People love free and love gifts. So you must offer a free gift doing this will get the traffic and attention that you want to your site. In addition, it will have them looking to see what you are about, what makes you different from others and also some will wonder why you can offer a free gift.

Here are some of the free stuffs you can offer at your blog or website:

1. Free ebooks: - People use search engine for information. And they love to download a FREE eBook which has a lot of informative contents. Offering a Free eBook is a great way to promote your blog or website. For this you can write your own eBook which has at least 5 pages. Simply you should go to Google and search about your niche. You will get a lot of contents on your searched topic. After that you should write a report about your topic and convert it in PDF format. Now you have got your free eBook and you just need to upload it on your blog or website. If you consider yourself that you are not a good writer, you can hire someone who writes for you.

2. Free software: - Plenty of internet user search for free software. You will get thousands of free software on whole net. You just need to search for PLR software or license-free software and upload at your website. You can also use your own software if you have an ability to create useful software.

3. Free SEO tools: - There are plenty of AdSense account holders and lot of other webmasters who want to learn about SEO. So, you should give them free SEO tools. Create your own SEO tool and release it for free, or search on Google for free SEO tools. Folks love SEO tips and SEO tricks. So, you should offer so many SEO ebooks.

4. Free funny videos: - You-Tube is the largest video holder website. You will get all type of videos at You-Tube. So, you need to make a list of funny videos of You-tube. And after that you should give links of those videos at your website. You can also use inspirational videos, motivational and your own business videos.

And any more you can think off.

By giving out free stuffs to people will help to generate traffic to your site and increase you earning (adsense) online. This is a secret which you must imbibe to generate traffic to your site and build authority in your niche.

CHAPTER 4.

HAVING AN ATTRACTIVE BLOG/WEBSITE THEME

For any website to be attractive, the appearance of the blog or website matters, greatly. Great premium theme will provide a huge head start towards creating a beautifully designed website.

There are many constituents that make up an attractive website theme. The Logo, Header Images, Colors, Fonts, Structures, and many all come together to make an attractive website or blog.

Here are a few tips for staying on the path to creating a beautiful WordPress site.

1. GREAT IMAGES

Images play a great role in making your website look attractive. Image can make or break the appearance of your site. If you plan to use images, don't go for free or cheap images because it will reflect poorly on your brand.

Great images are going to cost you more than a few bucks. If you don't have the budget for quality photography, there are a few options for finding good free imagery.

SOME PAID IMAGES RESOURCES:

1. **istockphoto.com; offers good and affordable images. They also offer one free image per week.**
2. **shutterstock.com; offers images similar to istock in terms of pricing and quality.**
3. **gettyimages.com; offer cream of the crop editorial images. They are fantastic. They are not cheap.**

FREE PHOTO RESOURCES:

1. **Unsplash – Free high quality photography, my personal favorite.**
2. **Use Instagram — A great way to get your own good looking images for free.**
3. **Flickr Creative Commons — you can find great images here. The usage conditions vary, but you generally need to give credit to the photographer.**
4. **stock.xchng: excellent free resource. You may have to do some digging on the site for quality images.**

2. FONT CHOICES

Use high quality font. Making great font choices is very important to the design, professionalism and above all else, the legibility of your site. If you want people to read your content — make it easy for them.

My font recommendations are Helvetica, Georgia or Ariel and the google font plugin to be use with your wordpress site or

Fontmeister — a promising font plugin for managing web fonts from multiple sources.

3. COLORS

Using best color combination for your website or blog is a very great way to make your site look attractive, but you must know that color can as well make your site look obscure. So choose color wisely. Remember to make wise color choices that match your brand.

4. YOUR LOGO

The logo of your website is also an important area to take very seriously. Remember a logo is more than just an icon at the top of your site — it's the face of your company.

In case you need great logo designer, I recommend logopond and you can also use fiverr. Keep it as simple as possible if you absolutely have to create your own logo without experience.

CHAPTER 5.

TELL INSPIRING STORIES TO CAPTIVATE READERS

Start with a setting: This sets the groundwork for the story. You will create the mood. Your first sentence should immediately pick interest and curiosity. Say something like "Guess what" or "Did you know". Choose something in your life that made an impact. Write as though your audience is with you. Make your audience become part of your story.

Tips on how to write an Inspiring and captivating blog post Stories.

1. **Decide your core point**. In order for a story to stick, you need to boil down the core of your message (ideally to a sentence or two). And do these before you write your story. What are you trying to say? What point do you want to get across to your reader? Make it simple and easy to understand.

How does your brand meet the needs of your audience better than other brands? Give examples.

Incorporate current affairs into your field. Write an article on a current affair about something people are searching for and merge it to a relevant area of your site. Be controversial. Mix and match theory with disbelief and see what you come up with. Use a content generator and infuse contradictory terms see what happens.

Brainstorm ideas. Instead of focusing on everything as you did in Freewriting focus on ideas. There will probably be something interesting you can use to write about.

2. **Determine the situation or setting**. Writers will know that every story needs a context or a setting where the story will play out. If done right, this will engage the reader emotionally and make them feel part of the story. People are always looking for something to connect to in a story, so make sure the context is detailed enough that they can find something to relate to on a personal level.

3. **Decide the problem**. Before writing the story, you should not only determine the point of the story, you also need to figure out what the problem is that you're trying to solve for the reader. Since the product or service you're writing about is designed (hopefully) to solve a problem or help the reader face a certain challenge, your story must connect the dots-from their problem, to your solution.

4. **Come to a turning point.** Every interesting story has a turning point in it called the climax, where the suspense of the story reaches its peak. Here, you must show the reader exactly how things change and how those changes will affect the final outcome of the story.

5. **Your Story Must Convert**. Since as a marketer, you're ultimately selling a product or service, the conversion piece of the story is the most important. This is where the story converges, and the solution (aka your product or service) is revealed.

Usually, this last piece is followed by the offer or call to action. But it should come naturally, and should never feel artificial.

Don't force it

Stories are a remarkable tool for any marketer wanting to get her message out into the world. But in order for stories to work their magic, they must be compelling and always, always authentic-people can sense a bogus story from miles away.

So what are you waiting for? Go tell your story today.

CHAPTER 6.

CRAFT COMPELLING HEADLINES

Compelling headlines largely contribute to the success of any blog post or article. It is only an attractive and captivating headline that arrests the attention of the readers. A headline that is confusing or dull will definitely not call for maximum page views.

Writing a compelling headline is all about creativity. You really have to think of something out of ordinary that will compel the readers to read your blog post or article.

Although they say content is still the king, but honest before people get to read your content, your compelling headline is what will direct people to read through your post or article. You need to lure them with a compelling, an interesting and irresistible headline. Try to put yourself in your readers' shoes while writing a headline, and ask yourself, that if you would have seen this line somewhere, would you make an effort to read the whole post or article.

Writing compelling headlines is a craft that one should learn and perfects with long years of practice. In fact, advertising agencies and newspapers have specialists dedicated to writing attention-grabbing headlines for news stories and ad campaigns.

Have you seen how hufftonpost craft their headlines? This is a skill that should be learnt to acquire.

TIPS TO A GREAT ATTENTION GRABBING HEADLINE

1. **Your headline should be huge and instantly noticeable.**
2. **The key to a successful headline is research.**
3. **Use compelling words on your headline.**

4. While it's true that people buy on emotion and justify with logic, don't forget about the second part - the logic.
5. There's no law or any kind of rule that says your headline must be a single line so don't be afraid to use multiple line long headlines if that's what you need.

There is a huge list of words that tempts your readers to click on "read more" button, such as:

- **The Secret of...**
- **Staggering Evidence of...**
- **Here's A Quick Way To...**
- **Ultimate...**
- **Awesome...**
- **Ideal...**
- **Mysterious...**
- **Extreme...**
- **Myths Debunked...**
- **Amazing...**
- **Worst... and many more.**

QUICK TIPS TO CONSTRUCT A BETTER HEADLINE.

- **Keep it short.**
- **Cover the main idea.**
- **Write the headline first.**
- **Benefit the reader.**
- **Add numbers.**
- **Create how-to headlines.**
- **Generate curiosity.**
- **Adopt proceeding formats.**
- **Use keywords.**

- Tell secrets.
- Make headlines funny.
- Ask a question.
- Be controversial.
- Captivate your audience.
- Make a promise of value and keep it.
- Use adjectives.

Now, all of us cannot aspire to be professional headline writers, but at least we can try. Here, then, are a few tips that you could try the next time you're racking your brains to come up with a headline with some punches.

- **While writing the title of the article, keep the target readers in mind.**
- **Browse through the other articles on similar topics and evaluate the kind of titles that attracts your attention the most.**
- **The headline should have the power to garner the reader's trust and faith.**
- **Also, make sure that the title is not too complicated. It has to be precise and to the point.**
- **Some all time favorite headline templates are given below:**
- **These are just some of the many popular headlines templates. Keep in mind, people mostly search for information online to find solutions to their problems. Therefore, a plain and blatant title will never have a good enough impact on the reader's mind.**

- If you are too confused about giving your article a suitable headline, then don't brood over it much. Start writing the article and after you finish it, then write the title of the article. This process works well for many as it becomes easier to create the headline after understanding the kind of direction the final article has taken.
- Last but not least, make the starting letters of all the words in your headline capital and also make the entire headline bold to make sure that it gets proper attention.

CHAPTER 7.

PLAN AND SCHEDULE YOUR POSTS

Plan is the major key to success in any business. Planning and scheduling your post is a key to success.

The Chinese provide says "if you fail to plan, you plan to fail".

So how do you want to make your post; daily, weekly or even monthly (not advisable)?

Planning in advance is more or less a commitment on your part as to what you intend to accomplish! This plan will actually help you stick to your schedule which of course should reflect a consistency you can live with and your readers can look forward to! With a bit of daily planning you can determine which days work best for you and your readers to post updates! As a rule holidays and weekends are NOT the best days for getting traffic to your blog since people typically have other obligations!

SO HOW MANY POSTS CAN YOU MAKE A DAY OR WEEK?

In order to be a successful blogger, you need to write content regularly. Some say, you should write every day. Well, that's probably where most people have problems with. I have to admit, it is not easy to write every day, especially when you have a lot of other things to do in your daily life.

Thankfully, we have WordPress. WordPress allows you to schedule your writings. In other words, you can schedule one day for writing. On that day, you write all the posts and schedule them to be published on specific dates.

Let's say you set every Monday as your writing day. So, on Mondays, you write 5 or 7 posts, more if you are in the mood. Schedule these posts to be published for that particular week - one post per day.

In the past, without a proper scheduling mechanism and tool, I would just blog whenever I had the time and mood. As such, please don't blog sparingly which may affect the traffic to your blog.

Today, with the help of this new Editorial Calendar plugin, I now have posts scheduled way into the future. I can go into my blog's back-end and add contents as and when I have the time - say perhaps every weekend or so. So try to use this plugin in your wordpress to ease you the pressure of writing and post almost every day.

Thanks to the Editorial Calendar Plugin. It certainly is an excellent plugin to have. It helps in planning all your posts.

Are you using WordPress' post scheduling feature? If not you really should. The Editorial Calendar plugin should be included as one of the must have plugin for all WordPress users.

My advice is that you don't rely on trying to pull all your content together at the last minute since the pressure and time will both compromise your quality! Knowing in advance which days you intend to update your site gives you the opportunity to prepare your next update in advance side stepping the need to rush your efforts! This will help ensure you post only quality content which of course is the foundation to any successful blog!

CHAPTER 8.

AVOID BLOGGERS BLOCK

Bloggers' block is a relatively new term given to the idea of having difficulty writing blog posts for no apparent reason. You can characterize this as that feeling when you know you should be writing something but you cannot seem to find the right words. Consequently, this leads to the non-creation of a blog post. People who blog for money or even just for recreation are not big fans of the bloggers' block. It is because bloggers' block is considered a hindrance to keeping an interesting and high-traffic blog.

It happens to the best of us. But you can't let it stop you. That is exactly why I've compiled some creative ways you can spark that Blogging muscle of yours.

Fortunately, there are a few tips you can follow to avoid bloggers' block. They are considerably easy because they really are some things you do on a normal day. You just happen to forget about them sometimes, which may even be one reason you are having bloggers' block.

Here they are:

1. **Read other blog posts and articles!**
2. **Research for your new posts.**
3. **Review your old posts.**
4. **Start a collection of blogs.**
5. **Watch some YouTube videos.**
6. **You could also start a blog post about not knowing what to blog about.**
7. **You could start a blog file or a document.**
8. **Last but not least is the timing aspect.**

Avoid the pattern of checking your email, surfing the web, watching videos, or checking your bank statement online whenever you are really deliberately trying to get a blog post out there for your readers to read. Checking and deleting email has hardly ever been a practice to spark your creative juices.

Bloggers' block is definitely not something you want to experience especially when you are trying to blog for money or for another important purpose. Hence, you have to double-up on your efforts not only in thinking of an interesting topic to blog about but also in finding ways to put your ideas into writing. This will help you create blog posts without any difficulty.

CHAPTER 9.

STAY MOTIVATED

One of the biggest roadblocks that stand between you and your goals is motivation. It is extremely hard to stay motivated when you have trouble reaching your goals, and it can be ever harder to get motivated if you have been trying to lose weight and get fit to no avail.

TIPS ON HOW TO GET AND STAY MOTIVATED

1- **Focus on Past Achievements**. Remember the accomplishments that you have had in the past. Dwell on them. Make them come to life again.

2- **Use Motivational Positive Affirmations**. Affirmations help you change your focus. While you are saying something positive to yourself it's all but impossible to think negative thoughts. Positive affirmations can motivate you to action in those times when you are feeling down.

3- **Stay Inspired**. Always know the reason behind what you want to do. If you want to run a marathon then knows what you are doing it for. Be very clear about your reason why.

4. **Set Realistic Goals**. In order to stay motivated, one of the first things that you will need to do is set goals that you feel you can achieve. One of the worst mistakes you could make would be to set a goal that you have no way of realistically reaching.

5. **Visualize the end result**. Visualize how you'll feel once you accomplish each goal. Make a to-do list for the things you'd like to do once you get this task out of the way. Maybe you'll take a mini vacation with your significant other, make an appointment to get a

massage, or take a day off and play golf. Hang that list where it will remind you frequently of the desired result.

6. **Reward yourself**. Set up small rewards for each goal you achieve. Staying motivated is a heck of a lot easier when you've got something exciting in the immediate future to look forward to.

7. **Find what drives you**. Are you driven by your own needs, by the need of your family, or by someone else? How about the needs of your clients? Find what drives you and then exploit it to stay motivated and focused. Write it down and post it at your work station where you will see it frequently throughout the day.

8. **Plan ahead**. Give yourself a set amount of time to complete each task and then move on. If you're not done before times up, save the task for the end of the day and reprioritize your to-do list for the following day.

9. **Divide responsibility**. Hold a family and/or team meeting to divide responsibilities throughout your household (and office) so you can free up your most valuable time to taking on the most high-impact actions.

10. **Remember why you do this**. Constantly be mindful of why you do what you do - it's one of the best ways to easily get and stay motivated.

11. **Use fear**. Think of what you could lose if you don't get the task at hand completed. Analyze what's at stake and let the fear of losing these valuable things pump you into getting motivated!

Follow these tips will help you get and stay motivated and you will continue to move closer to achieving your goals. Remember, it's about staying focused and disciplined, taking many positive steps forward while minimizing or eliminating the backwards steps, and committing to doing what it takes to get you where you want to be.

You can always get to your goal if you follow those steps and remain focused.

CHAPTER 10.

CONNECT WITH YOUR READER

If you have a blog or you create content online and you are trying to build an audience then you need to learn how you can best communicate with that audience.

FOCUS

Everything that you write or create needs to be focused on your audience. After all they are the people who will be reading or watching it and therefore you should always be providing what they need and offering them the help that they will find beneficial. It's not about you it's about your readers what they want.

Imagine that you are a reader and think about the types of content that you would find really helpful and valuable. Try to put yourself in your readers' shoes.

Give Freely

If you want to build a responsive audience then you need to learn to give freely. I have often heard people say that if they give too much away and if they share too much valuable information then no one will purchase anything from them. If you give away some of your secrets then why would someone buy your product?

In reality the more you give the more likely people are to purchase from you. The more they will trust you and respect you. The more value they will receive from you and they will want more!

Understand

Another important aspect is to fully understand where your readers are coming from. What is their perspective? What position are they coming from - a novice or a professional? Perhaps you target a wide range and your readers come from varying levels of expertise. Make sure that when you write you add value to all of your readers.

LISTENING

Connecting with anyone is about listening. Learning to listen what your readers think about things and what their opinions are is really important for you to fully understand where they are coming from. It also enables you to better understand what their difficulties are and what they actually want. This is important when it comes to producing products that your readers will find most beneficial.

BE POSITIVE IN YOUR ARTICLES.

Being too negative turns people off unless it is for a valid reason or you want to put a useful point across that will help your readers. Use words that inspire people to take action.

WRITE FOR YOUR READERS.

Try to imagine being in their shoes while reading your article. What will their response be? How will they react? Are the likely to visit your website? Will they be hungry to buy your products after reading it?

WRITE LIKE HOW YOU TALK.

This is one of the easiest ways to connect with your readers and make your articles an interesting read. Of course, this doesn't mean your article is disorganized, but you do want to write your articles as if you were talking to your friend across a coffee table. Readers will connect better with you this way.

Building connections and relationships with prospects and readers of your blog or content that you write online is the foundation for a successful business. If you don't build strong relationships you are unable to build trust and if you don't build trust then people are more unwilling to spend money.

CHAPTER 11.

WRITE IN THE PERFECT ENVIRONMENT

Creating perfect Blog writing Environment is very simple and requires you determine the best time and the good atmosphere you think will be good for you to think and write captivating blog post.

Let us consider various ways by which you can create conducive writing environment.

THIS IS WHAT YOU SHOULD CONSIDER:

1. STANDING OR SITTING:

Some think that it seems that standing actually is healthier and aids focus, but I prefer sitting on my couch thinking and writing. You what do you think is best for you? The point is that you want to adopt a posture that leads to maximum focus. Sitting sometimes helps to remove distraction from writing you captivating blog post.

2. MUSIC:

I've been experimenting with music variations for years. I've found that a piano arrangement is the mother's milk of creativity. It's easy to slip into the zone and pound out page after page of copy.

Research says that music works best for people who need a high level of stimulation to focus. These are the folks that need the TV, radio, kids scurrying under foot, and an open magazine to concentrate. Low level of arousal people need complete silence. Most of us fall in between. I like my radio on while writing my blog post, what about you?

Test to see what works for you.

3. PRIMING THE PUMP

I often watch some videos before writing. The inspiration rubs off on me and I can channel the feeling into my writing. I have a friend that can sit down and start writing immediately without watching any video.

If you have difficulty "getting started" think about ways you can "prime the pump." Read an inspirational short story, watch a video, or remember a time when you operated at your peak. Now channel that into the spark you need to get going.

4. DISTRACTIONS

You can use a text editor like Byword to blank out your screen except for text. I use these tricks religiously to keep destructive distractions at arm's length. For me, this includes Twitter, Facebook, email.

5. EQUIPMENT

I focus on my Mouse, Monitor, and Keyboard. This helps me to concentrate more on the assignment I have at hand.

6. SOFTWARE

I'm somewhat of a software junkie and I have tested dozens of applications. As you would expect, software choice is based on the personality and style of the writer. So there isn't a perfect tool for everyone.

I use Google Docs because of the auto save having my document automatically available in the Cloud. ByWord is a close second because it helps eliminate distractions and has configurable paper colors that helps ease eye strain.

From here, I cut and paste my blog posts directly into WordPress. I never write in WordPress. When I've attempted it, one of two things happen: I hit the "publish" instead of update or inexplicably lose everything when the software seizes up. So I write in the Docs first and paste when I'm finished.

7. LOCATION

My best place to write is in my home office, behind a closed-door, with the headphones on. This arrangement is easy and leaves little room for procrastination. Just go in, shut the door, and start typing.

Find a place that works for you and stick with it.

No Hard and Fast Rule Other Than…

I'm curious. What is your perfect blog writing environment?

CHAPTER 12.

HOW DO I WRITE GREAT BLOG POSTS

With millions of blogs posts fighting for readership online and with thousands more being created every day. You need to make yours blog postings stand out above the rest. Here are some suggestions for making your blog posts stand out from the crowd.

1. The first thing someone reads is the post title so **write each post title that grabs the reader's attention**. Your title should both wet the reader's interest and be informative. Do not write "Blog Writing Advice"; instead, say "The Best Kept Secret to Improving Your Blog Writing." The longer titles have the advantage of describing in detail what your post is about. 8 to 12 words work best.

2. **Keep sentences short and clear**. A little goes a long way. Readers are busy people and they will not spend hours reading fluff. Use strong language. Start a new paragraph every few sentences, and limit each post to 250 words, if possible. If you cannot write it in under 250 words, split it into two entries.

3. **Break up the text**. Use numbered lists, bullet points, and subheadings to make your posts easy to scan. A lot of white space on the page is a good thing, It allows your reader to take mental breaks and lets the knowledge soak in. This technique puts some distance between your writing and all those distractions like the constant clutter of banner ads and side text.

4. **Keep current**. No one wants to read old news. Your job is to keep up to date so your readers do not have to themselves. Read newspapers. Search the web for references. If you write a blog about blogging, subscribe to Google News Alerts using keywords related to the field, such as blogs, podcasting, instant messaging, business letters, memos, and business reports, so you will always be well informed. Posting items from last month or last year will lose your reader's interest.

5. **Be bold**. Being timid is an easy path to anonymity. Do not be afraid to create and state your opinions. There are some situations in which objectivity rules. But you have to give people a reason to read your blog and not the person next door. Be accurate. If you make a statement, be prepared to back it up. Know what your sources are and quote them accurately. Do not post misinformation.

6. **Contribute to the conversation**. Links are great but then what? Do not just post links to the same tired sites, offer your reader something new. Contribute to the conversation. Your goal is to be the site to which everyone else is linking so you had better have something to say.

7. **Stay focused**. Once you have defined the theme of your blog, stay on it. A blog about sky diving has no business posting about the latest innovation in swimming. Such a deviance will only confuse your readership and destroy your virtual authority.

8. **Use key words liberally**. Keywords are keys to your success online. They harness your blog's search engine potential when you fill your title and post with effective keywords that helps interested readers find your page in the amongst all the others.

9. **Be consistent**. Keep a schedule and stick to it. Post frequently at least several times per week if you want to increase your potential of attracting new readers. If you let your blog languish for weeks without updates your audience will move on to fresher blogs. Maintaining an informative blog that people want to read takes hard work and good writing skills. Find what makes your writing unique and flaunt it for all it is worth.

10. **Make it sound lively**. Reading your blog posts must not feel like listening to a sermon during Sunday mass. If you want your readers to stick around, you must not only educate them but you need to entertain them as well. Use friendly, conversational tone all the time. Offer interesting stories, inject humor, and engage your readers by asking them relevant questions from time to time.

CHAPTER 13.

15 GREAT BLOG POST IDEAS

Creating a blog, either for pleasure or in the hope of making earnings, is an interesting prospect. More and more people are deciding to start one in their own specialized area. Interestingly, many people jump straight into it with more thought to the concept than to the topic and the posts. Thus, before you start your blog, I would like to challenge you to sit down and write out at least 50 post ideas, and write on not less than 10 of them.

TIPS OF GREAT BLOG POST IDEAS

Content marketing is continuing to play an increasingly important part in marketing your business effectively.

There's only one small problem. You need to have a steady and consistent supply of content for it to work... and how can you come up with enough content marketing ideas to keep that flow going?

What content can you continue to create that will attract the right traffic for your business, and bring new leads and customers through your door?

That's where this article comes in, and it's actually far simpler than you might believe.

Here are fourteen awesome ways to keep ideas flowing into your content marketing funnel, and allow you to build an increasing level of online visibility and traffic for your business in the months and years ahead.

1. KEYWORD RESEARCH

Did you know sites like eHow.com have built much of their success on keyword research? Their content is largely created on what their research tells them people are looking for online. You can simply employ the same strategy. Make use of Google planner if you cannot afford paid like Long tail Pro.

2. QUORA

This is another place you can generate thousands of ideas for your blog post. Quora has a huge amount of potential for idea generation. It contains queries on a ton of different topics - simply find your niche, and look through the queries to discover what people are trying to find out about.

3. CUSTOMER QUESTIONS

Your own customer support is an invaluable source of ideas because you hear straight from the horse's mouth what information your customers and prospects are looking for.

4. BLOG COMMENTS

Similar to the above, comments on your blog enable you to listen directly to your marketplace, and you can then create content to respond to those needs.

5. OTHER BLOGS IN YOUR NICHE

By reading other blogs within your niche, you can get some great ideas for your own posts, and gain further inspiration from the comments they receive. For example, you might be able to flesh out a topic they briefly touched on in their post, or approach it from a new angle.

6. TWITTER

Search Twitter and discover what's happening in your own niche. As well as comments you'll see links to a lot of other content that could help inspire your own.

7. HOT TOPICS

What are the main topics of conversation in your industry right now, from your customer's point of view? What are their primary concerns, right now? Use their concern to build a powerful blog post.

8. How-To Tutorials

How-to type content remains very popular, and providing such content is a great way in which you can immediately gain authority and trust with someone. You'll also find people get referred to your tutorial from others who have benefited from your advice.

9. Items in the News

What's in the news right now that affects customers in your niche? Alternatively, how could you adapt and apply key news stories to your business? Tapping into the conversation already in your customer's mind can be a powerful way to capture their attention and reach audiences who haven't come across you before.

10. Previous Content

Content you have created before can easily form the basis of new content. For example, you can approach it from a different angle, or use a different media. A blog post written previously can form the basis of a video on YouTube. Topics briefly touched on before can be expanded into completely new content items.

11. List-From Content

This article is a list-form article - content formed on the basis of creating a list about something. What lists could you create of relevance for your own potential customers?

12. STAY ALERT!

Train your brain to take advantage of new ideas as they arise. Opportunities for new content are all around you! Start carrying a notebook and pen around with you, or use your smartphone. Jot down new ideas whenever they arise... your brain will get used to it, and supply you with increasing numbers of ideas to pick from.

13. INTERVIEW SOMEONE

Who is well known and familiar to your customers, and who has relevance to your business (or how can you make what they do relevant)? You'll be surprised at how willing most people are to be interviewed. Just make a list of questions, and record the conversation... use Skype or a Google Hangout.

14. INTERVIEW YOURSELF!

Either ask someone to interview you, or interview yourself. This gives a great opportunity to display your expertise, gain credibility with your audience, and reach new audiences you wouldn't otherwise reach. For example, someone interviewing you could make the interview available to their own list.

15. Another great suggestion I've picked up is try splitting your posts into different types for your area. For instance, if you're playing to post three times a week you might have Information Monday, How-To Wednesday and Review Friday. Then you just need to ponder on about 20 ideas under each one of these.

For a blog on house building you might have some Information posts on different types of architecture, How-To numerous renovation projects, and Review the top tools of the trade. This will make it much easier to think of topics, and figure out what to write.

So, using these tips, it should only take you a little bit of research to come up with 50 topics for your blog. This is time that's not wasted. Once you have completed this, take at least 10 of those topics, write up the post and save them as drafts. You'll thank me for this later. Trust me.

Chapter 14.

Elements of Engaging Blog Post Ideas

With the ongoing proliferation of content in various forms around the web, it's becoming ever more essential to ensure the content you create engages the attention of your intended audience and stands out from the crowd.

What causes you to engage with a particular piece of content above others vying for your attention?

What is it that maintains that engagement? Or, conversely, what causes you to lose interest and click away?

What aspects of the content encourage you to share it with others?

If you're searching for something online, what encourages you to click through to one result above another?

As you know, there's a no shortage of competing content out there, all pleading for our time and attention.

To rise above the noise and ensure your own content engages your intended audience is no mean feat. But with a few key elements in mind, it's certainly achievable.

So what helps create such engaging content? What ensures a piece of content not only grabs your attention in the first place, but holds it and makes an imprint on your mind?

Of course, we all have our own individual likes and dislikes, and so I surveyed a group of people interested in content marketing on just these questions. Based on the answers I received, the following list represents what may be considered to be some essential elements of engaging, attention-grabbing content.

KEY ELEMENTS TO BEAR IN MIND

1: AN ATTENTION-GRABBING TITLE

Whether your content is an article, a blog post, a video, audio recording, or whatever, the title plays an absolutely essential role. It needs to both ensure your content stands out from the crowd, and appeals to your intended audience.

It should:

- Be specific: what exactly does the content offer?
- Be intriguing: how can you arouse the curiosity of those you are hoping to attract, so they're almost compelled to click through?
- Offer a solution: where there's a problem, there's a desire or need for a solution - how can your title tap into that?

2: DELIVER ON ITS PROMISE

Have you ever clicked through on a piece of content only to find it doesn't provide what you thought it would?

It's essential to deliver on the promise of your title for the following key reasons:

- Once you've engaged someone's attention in the first place, you then need to maintain their attention in order for the content to ultimately benefit you. For example, you're looking for someone to visit your website, share the content with others, link up with you on social media, and so on, as well as generally raise the online profile of you and your business.
- If someone is clicking through to your content from Google, and then rapidly clicking back to the search engine results to click through somewhere else, it tells Google something about how to rank your content. If your content is not delivering what their search users are looking for, its rank will deteriorate over time. On the other hand, if your content grabs their attention and holds it, it can only benefit the ranking of your content.

3: MEET A NEED

Your content largely exists for one reason only - to grab the attention of potential prospects for your business.

Your content must therefore meet a need that audience has in order to grab their attention and engage with them.

What are the needs of your marketplace? What problems are they facing? What questions frequently arise? What are they looking for assistance with or information about?

There are various ways to find out, such as direct feedback from existing customers and prospects, social media, forums, industry publications, and so on.

4: AUTHENTICITY

People like to connect with people like themselves. Show through your content that you are a real person just like them, with real thoughts, opinions, feelings, and ideas.

Sure, you'll turn some people away, but try to please everyone and you end up pleasing no-one. Instead, be authentic and open, and you'll attract an audience who will resonate strongly with you, engage effectively with your content, and be very responsive because of the connection you have with them. And a smaller but responsive audience is far more valuable than a larger but indifferent one.

5: ORIGINALITY - OFFER A UNIQUE PERSPECTIVE

If your content is simply a rehashed version of similar content elsewhere, it's not going to grab anyone's attention or stand out from the crowd.

Instead, offer them the benefit of your own unique knowledge and experience, and put your own unique stamp on your content.

6: IMPROVE LIVES

Okay, it's not quite in the same league as discovering a cure for cancer or eradicating poverty, but none-the-less your content should aim to improve the lives of your audience.

By helping others through your content, you make your content memorable for them. They will also remember you, and more readily connect with you, whether by signing up to your email list, connecting over social media, or looking out for your content in future and referring you to others.

7: THOUGHT-PROVOKING

By making your audience think, even if they don't always agree with you, you'll engage more easily with them, stick in their minds for longer and raise your profile. Don't be afraid to challenge your audience or go against the grain: controversy sells.

8: FLOWS EASILY

Unless your content flows well, people will rapidly disengage and click away.

Take time to carefully review every piece of content, or have someone else go through it for you and highlight any sticking points or parts they don't understand. You'll be surprised what you can improve by leaving your content for a few days after creating it, and then carefully reviewing it.

Ensure you are using correct spelling and grammar. Basic spelling mistakes, typos and poor use of English reflects badly on you and gives a poor impression.

Use effective formatting, such as bullet points, and short paragraphs for easy online reading.

Ensure you use language your intended audience will understand. Avoid the use of jargon that is only like to alienate those you are hoping to attract.

9: Engage Emotionally

Various studies have shown that emotions are key drivers for human activity. That includes choosing whether to engage with or disengage from your content, and whether or not to share your content with others. Often such decisions are entirely subconscious.

Content that becomes viral nearly always makes some key emotional connection with its audience.

Speed is also important, and is one reason why images are so prolific on social media and generally have higher levels of viral activity than other types of content.

Try to engage emotionally with your audience within the first few seconds of them finding your content, and you'll both hold their attention for longer and increase the benefits your content delivers for your business.

Of course, it won't always be possible to incorporate all these elements into every piece of content you create. But by trying to incorporate as many as possible, you will undoubtedly create more engaging, attention-grabbing content, and improve the results you achieve from your content marketing activities.

CHAPTER 15.

HOW TO IMPROVE THE QUALITY OF YOUR BLOG CONTENT

The most common problem with a lot of web articles these days is that they don't make any sense. I've seen a lot of copies that are just waste of my precious time. This is because a lot of article writers do not really care about giving their audience what they deserve; these people are just concern in using their articles to add keyword-power to their websites. If you're one of them, let me tell you that publishing senseless articles will not help you succeed in the online arena.

So, start improving the quality of your articles. Here's how you can do that:

1. **Go with topics that are recent and in-demand**. First thing to do is to find a topic to discuss that is extremely interesting to your target audience. Do a keyword research or simply ask your readers to send in their topic requests. Go with topics that are relatively new and those that have direct impact to the lives of your readers.

2. **Do your homework**. Even if you're very familiar with your chosen topics, it's still recommended that you do your research. This is to make sure that you'll obtain the freshest, complete information that your readers are looking for. Aside from checking out RSS feeds, relevant blogs, and websites, it will also help if you interview experts in this particular niche. If needed, do some experiments and get first-hand experience.

3. **Plan your content**. Organize your materials before you start writing. You can do this by simply creating an outline that contains all the information that you're going to discuss in your copies.

4. **Use Strong headlines**. People make the decision whether to read an article or not based on the headline. Make it juicy, or at least use it to communicate a worthwhile usage of time, otherwise people are likely to skip it.

When you follow all the points mentioned above, I know for sure your content will be improved and please do some more research on this by looking at some websites in your niche.

CONCLUSION

I hope you enjoyed reading all the tips and tricks I shared in this book. Make sure to abide by it all and you will see real success just as I have seen.

This isn't the end of the journey but the beginning of another. Remember, do your homework before writing your content, research is important. If you don't have authoritative information, readers won't just walk away, they'll run away. Plan your content by jotting down key ideas and information, and then you WRITE.

The most important advice I can give you before we part ways, "Just Do It." Don't procrastinate, don't say tomorrow or next week, get up, open your laptop/computer, open a word processor and start writing away.

Anyways I hope everyone is successful in their endeavors. Till next time!

CAN I ASK A FAVOUR?

If you enjoyed this book, found it useful or otherwise then I'd really appreciate it if you would post a short review on Amazon. I do read all the reviews personally so that I can continually write what people are wanting.

If you'd like to leave a review then please CLICK HERE.

Thanks for your support!

BONUS CHAPTER

Tips to Starting Your Own Kindle Publishing Business

As a token of my appreciation for purchasing this book, I have decided to add an additional chapter which I think will immensely help you to get started with your own publishing business. As always don't forget to rate and comment and tell me how you liked this book!

TIP 1: PICK YOUR NICHE

When choosing a topic for your book, find a niche that's large enough to generate sufficient sales, while still small enough that you can dominate it. To identify such a niche, generate a list of keywords that best describes your own expertise and then search for books on those topics in the Kindle Store. Stick to UK versions if your book will mainly appeal to natives, otherwise base your analysis on Amazon.com. Start with quite a broad search phrase and narrow it whenever you encounter too many competitors.

For example, you might start by searching for plain "Raspberry Pi" if you're interested in writing about this cheap computing phenomenon.

Sort your results by popularity and then open the top one. When I tried this it was, hardly surprisingly, the official Raspberry Pi User Guide (co-written by Gareth Halfacree of this parish). Its ranking at just over 5,000 suggests sales of at least 15 copies per day at a royalty of £6 per copy, or some £90 per day, £30,000+ per annum from UK sales. Not bad.

Repeat this process by moving down the search list. In this example, the second-most popular title generates around £22 per day and the next few £16, £5 and £2.50 respectively. You'll notice a familiar pattern here, where two-thirds of the revenues go to the most popular title and more than 80% to the top two together. Carry on down some way and you'll very soon be among books that required considerable effort to produce but are selling around one copy a week.

You conclude that there's clearly money to be made from an enthusiastic audience eager to learn, especially considering that you've only looked at UK Kindle sales so far, and many of these titles will be available globally in multiple formats. But you also see plenty of titles in this niche that have failed to make any impact at all.

TIP 2: PUBLISH A GREAT BOOK

Having located your market niche, you'll need to produce the goods. Remember to closely base your actual title on the keywords you researched, since this is how your audience will find you on Amazon. This may sound obvious, but if you were to compare the best-selling books in any particular category with those that languish in the virtual equivalent of a box under the bed, you'll notice big differences in quality – the most popular books will be professionally presented, complete and well written.

Having a copy editor run through your book at least once before publishing is an excellent investment, and unless you're a graphic artist you should also hire a cover designer. Many potential readers get no further than the thumbnail, and since the ebook shops don't separate titles into ones published by industry giants and home-produced efforts, your "Guide to Microsoft Office" needs to look the business when viewed alongside similar titles from the big guns.

Fortunately, neither copy-editing nor cover design are particularly expensive: just make sure you pick contractors who are qualified and competent, rather than automatically plumping for the cheapest.
Your book will succeed or fail based on the reviews it receives, so producing a professional package will go a long way to satisfying the fickle ebook audience.

Tip 3: Get the price right

Professor Brian Cox discovered just how fickle ebook purchasers can be when he contributed to a book that explains how the universe will end. This was part of a series called "Shorts", and managed to distil a complex subject down into an understandable format for 99p. The problem according to most Amazon reviewers was that he did this in a measly 20 pages. You might think having the end of the universe explained in layman's terms for less than a quid is a bargain, but many Kindle readers disagreed, measuring value based purely on pages per penny.

The rules of print paperback production don't apply to ebooks

This said, the rules of print paperback production don't apply to ebooks, since readers can't judge a Kindle book by its heft in their hand – anything above about 50 pages will usually be considered a reasonable read for a non-fiction book.

When you plan your book, then, consider the right size. I planned to sell my 200-pager for £4.99, but it might have been wiser to split it into four 50-page chunks on different aspects of the topic, then sell each for £1.49. This will work better for some subject matter than others; just remember that the ebook format frees you from any specific page count.

Once your book has been released, experiment with pricing. Mine has dropped from £4.99 at launch to a current price of £1.99. I left it at the high price for a few months, then tested the way changes affect revenue by dropping it to £1.49 over Easter, and finally raised it a little again. Surprisingly, I make much the same money from the book whatever its price, since roughly when I halve the price I double sales. But higher sales bring a better ranking and more reviews, both of which increase credibility and conversion rate, so while the revenue stream may be the same either way, I'd expect sales to last longer at a lower price point.

TIP 4: MULTIPLE MEDIA

Writers and publishers have barely started breaking free of the constraints imposed by traditional printing methods, and I expect to see a lot of innovation in connecting together different media over the next few years. Our mythical Raspberry Pi book, for example, might contain links to supporting YouTube tutorials that show how to translate the principles it describes into practice.

For now, one effective way to maximise the return on your writing is to also publish your ebook as a paperback. Print-on-demand services such as Lulu and Amazon's own CreateSpace enable you to offer a paperback version, which can be delivered as quickly as a traditionally published book, since Amazon keeps a small stock. Actually, to Amazon there's no difference between a Lulu-printed book and one from HarperCollins, which regrettably means that it will take the same big chunk of its cover price.

On the other hand, linking your paperback and Kindle book together will drive sales of both, since reviews are amalgamated into a single listing that inevitably makes the ebook look a bargain.

You can also buy copies of your own print book at cost (around £3 each for a 200-page paperback) to sell directly through your own channels, which enables you to keep a much larger slice of the profit. Also consider offering a PDF version of the book direct from your own website, whose cost to you is close to zero.

Tip 5: Find an Audience

It isn't enough to write an excellent book, publish it and hope for the best. If you've done your research and picked a good title, some readers searching on Amazon will certainly find you, but you need to supplement them with direct traffic from other sources if you're to make the most of your hard work. One approach is to sell your book directly as I just mentioned: if you have an established website with an appropriate audience, consider both selling the printed version and including links to the Kindle version.

You can also tap an existing community for valuable marketing information. I asked the customers of my retail craft business what they wanted covered in my book and was surprised by their replies: my book was all the better for their direct input. I promised a free copy of the ebook to all who contributed, then emailed to ask for their reviews once they'd read it. Frankly I was disappointed by that response, as the 100 contributors wrote only a couple of reviews between them. For my next book I'll be looking at strategies for getting more reviews that are available on publication day, since these strongly influence sales.

Google+ recently introduced "Communities", a feature that allows like-minded people to discuss related topics in a far more sophisticated manner than Facebook's Pages or Groups. If you were writing a book about, say, Raspberry Pi, there are several communities devoted to that device you can join – contribute to them and you earn the right to gently promote your book from time to time.

My experience was that income from KDP Select lending outstripped combined revenues from the Apple, Barnes & Noble and Kobo stores

Communities are also a great place to learn more about your subject – including self-publishing itself (check out the APE:

Authors, Publishers, Entrepreneurs) – particularly in fast-moving fields. I think Communities may prove to be the killer feature of Google+, with much of the social network's interaction taking place in these super-forums. I'll also be more actively building an email list for my next book – which, after all, is what I'd do for any other product or business.

TIP 6: STICK TO ONE PLATFORM

This one's simple: don't bother with any other ebook platform until you've nailed Kindle Direct Publishing (KDP). Even then, think carefully about whether your time will be well spent – I've described previously the tortuous hoops I was put through to get my title published on Apple's iBookstore, Barnes & Noble's Nook and the Kobo store. That was an utter waste of time I could otherwise have spent either promoting sales on KDP or writing another book.

Perhaps I shouldn't have been so surprised since – in the case of Apple's devices – readers have the option to use the Kindle app rather than iBooks. The market for Nook and Kobo books seems tiny compared with that for Kindle, and I'd only bother if you've exhausted all avenues to increase sales on Amazon's platform.

Sticking exclusively to KDP qualifies your title for the KDP Select programme, which enables you to offer your book free for a specified number of days in order to drum up interest and generate reviews. Perhaps more significantly still, it means your ebook can be borrowed by Kindle-owning members of Amazon's Prime programme. You'll be paid each time someone borrows your book, and while the amount isn't huge (around £1 per loan), my experience was that income from KDP Select lending outstripped combined revenues from the Apple, Barnes & Noble and Kobo stores.

TIP 7: ONE NICHE, MULTIPLE TITLES

I haven't tested this tip yet, but I've come across it many times during my research. It makes sense that if a reader likes your book they may well enjoy other books by you – but only so long as they cover a similar topic. This works with fiction too: I'd buy anything by Terry Pratchett within the genre for which he's famous, but if he published a book of romantic fiction I'd be off like a shot.

If your interests are too wide to accommodate within one genre, then take another tip from fiction and consider using a pen name for your other titles. However, from a business point of view, you ought to stick to a single niche, allowing you to offer book bundles, and even give away the first title in a series to drive sales of the rest. You can also cross-promote books, and the more titles you have, the more effective this will be.

Using these tips, I've made more money (both in revenue and profit) from one book over three months than from my entire stable of mobile apps in a year, and with far less time invested. Not surprisingly, then, I'll be experimenting further with self-publishing for profit over the coming year, and will keep you up to date.

Made in the USA
Middletown, DE
22 June 2018